Everything You Need to Know About *Food Poisoning*

Food poisoning can be dangerous, even fatal, but it is often preventable.

Everything You Need to Know About Food Poisoning

Mick Isle

The Rosen Publishing Group, Inc.
New York

To Myroka for the three hour supermarket forays and to Edi J. for the kitchen company

Published in 2001 by The Rosen Publishing Group, Inc.
29 East 21st Street, New York, NY 10010

Library of Congress Cataloging-in-Publication Data

Isle, Mick.
Everything you need to know about food poisoning / by Mick Isle.—1st ed.
p.; cm. — (The need to know library)
Includes bibliographical references and index.
ISBN 0-8239-3396-2 (library binding)
1. Food poisoning—Juvenile literature. 2. Food—Microbiology—Juvenile literature. [1. Food poisoning. 2. Food handling—Safety measures.] [DNLM: 1. Food Poisoning—Popular Works. 2. Food Handling—Popular Works. WC 268 I82e 2001] I. Title. II. Series.
RC143 .I83 2001
615.9'54—dc21

00-012610

Manufactured in the United States of America

Contents

Introduction

*J*ackson had a great time at the end-of-year school picnic. Winter that year had been long and cold. Then miraculously, the day before the picnic, the temperature shot up to almost eighty degrees. Jackson worked up a ferocious appetite playing Frisbee, and he ended up eating four hamburgers.

A few hours later, Jackson felt a headache coming on. He also started feeling queasy, as if he was going to throw up. He wondered if the sudden change in temperature had weakened his resistance. Was he experiencing the beginnings of the flu? Or perhaps he had caught some virus that was going around.

Food poisoning can often be avoided by cooking, preparing, and handling food in a safe manner.

When the picnic was over, Jackson went home and went straight to bed. In the middle of the night, he woke up with an incredible stomachache. The next thing he knew, he was dashing to the bathroom to throw up. He spent most of the night hunched over the toilet. And although his mouth was really dry, even a glass of water made him feel nauseous. He had never had a case of the flu or had caught a virus like this before.

Food poisoning is good at disguising itself. Like Jackson, many people mistake a mild case of food poisoning for a virus or the flu. Yet every year, millions of

Americans suffer from various forms of food poisoning. Food poisoning, or illnesses caused by food, occurs when tiny living bacteria or viruses contaminate the food that you eat. Bacteria grow and multiply in food that is improperly prepared, stored, cooked, or frozen.

Although food poisoning can make you very sick—and, in some cases, can prove dangerous to the point of being fatal—it can most often be avoided by learning about food safety and taking proper precautions when handling food. In this book, we will explore the various types of food poisoning, how to identify and treat them, and most important, how not to get food poisoning in the first place.

Chapter 1

What Is Food Poisoning?

As we saw in the introduction, in most cases, food poisoning is caused by eating food—or drinking unpasteurized milk and juices or untreated water—that contain certain kinds of bacteria or viruses. These can show up in almost any type of food, but particularly risky are meats, fish, poultry, eggs, unpasteurized dairy products, and any kind of dishes made with these ingredients. When raw or improperly packaged, cooked, or stored, these foods can become breeding grounds for germs. Once you have eaten such food, the organisms continue to grow inside you. In doing so, they cause an infection. Furthermore, some bacteria create toxins, or poisons, that can spread through food. These toxins can also cause you to get sick.

Seafood Is the Biggest Cause of Food Poisoning

In August 2000, the Center for Science in the Public Interest (CSPI), a consumer group that researches health and other issues, released a report on food poisoning in the United States. It found that seafood is the biggest cause of food poisoning in the United States, having caused 237 outbreaks since 1990. Eggs were the second most frequent cause, responsible for 170 outbreaks (mostly salmonella). Third was beef (ninety-one outbreaks, forty of which came from hamburger meat), and fourth were fruits and vegetables (eighty-one outbreaks, most of which were caused by alfalfa sprouts and lettuce). The CSPI has criticized the U.S. government for not doing enough to "clean up" these foods.

Food that is contaminated can be dangerous, especially to those with weaker resistance, such as very young and very old people. Food poisoning leads to an average of 9,000 deaths per year. Each year, food poisoning also causes fever, diarrhea, vomiting, and stomach cramps in nearly 80 million Americans. This means that, over the course of a year, close to one-third of all Americans suffer from some form of food poisoning.

The Most Common Causes of Food Poisoning

There are quite a few types of bacteria and viruses that can cause food poisoning. Here are some of the most common:

Salmonella and *Campylobacter*—two types of bacteria that are quite similar. Both are found in warm-blooded animals such as poultry, cattle, and pigs and may show up in raw meat, eggs, or unpasteurized dairy products such as milk and cheeses.

Listeria—a recently discovered bacteria that thrives in soil and in animals' intestines. It can appear in the types of foods listed in the *Salmonella* entry.

Calicivirus (or Norwalk-like virus)—very common cause of food poisoning, characterized by lots of vomiting. It is believed that the virus passes from one infected person to another. Infected kitchen workers, for example, can contaminate a sandwich if the virus is on their hands.

Clostridium perfringens—bacteria found in the foods mentioned in the *Salmonella* entry as well as in vegetables and herbs that come into contact with soil. It usually shows up in soups, stews, and sauces made with meat, poultry, or fish that are stored improperly.

Clostridium botulinum—found basically everywhere, including in water and soil. However, when conditions such as a lack of oxygen and low acidity occur, these bacteria grow quickly, producing toxins. These bacteria can show up in meat, poultry, fish, and vegetables that are improperly canned, preserved, or cooked and are then left at room temperature too long. The type of food poisoning that can result—botulism—is rare but often deadly.

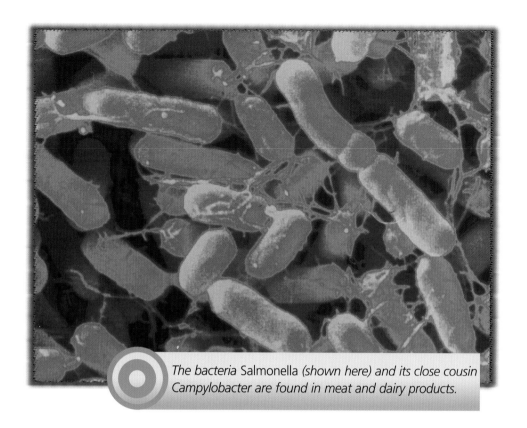

The bacteria Salmonella *(shown here) and its close cousin* Campylobacter *are found in meat and dairy products.*

Staphylococcus (staph)—usually found on human skin and in the nose and throat. When you cough on food or touch it with unwashed hands, the bacteria can contaminate the food. When food that spoils easily is not refrigerated properly, staph multiply. In doing so, they create toxins that are very resistant to heat.

Vibrio parahaemolyticus—bacteria found in seawater that can contaminate raw seafood such as oysters, clams, crabs, and shrimp.

Dinoflagellate—type of algae found in the ocean. It can create a toxin that affects the human nervous system. Shellfish such as mussels, clams, oysters, and scallops sometimes eat this poisonous algae.

Shigella—bacteria that thrives in areas with poor sanitary conditions. It is common among travelers in developing countries who eat contaminated food.

E. coli (Escherichia coli)—bacteria commonly found in untreated water and raw meats, particularly ground beef. It produces toxins that can infect the intestines and create an illness commonly known as traveler's diarrhea.

How Do You Get Food Poisoning?

Most often, people get food poisoning when they eat food that is contaminated with bacteria or bacteria-produced toxins. However, in some cases, such as salmonella and shigella poisoning, poisoning can occur from drinking contaminated or untreated water.

Campylobacter poisoning can be acquired by being in close contact with sick people or animals. *E. coli* poisoning can be caught from family members who have

Know What You're Eating

◉ Make sure that you know what you're putting in your mouth. There are countless cases of people munching on mushrooms that they thought were harmless, and dying because they were in fact eating poisonous mushrooms.

◉ It's also important that food is properly prepared. In Japan, a great delicacy is blowfish, which, when properly prepared, leaves you with a pleasant tingling sensation in your mouth. If prepared improperly, you could end up paralyzed, or even dead.

been recently infected by the bacteria, or by traveling in areas in which *E. coli* is endemic (that is, always present in the region). You can even get it from diving into a swimming pool filled with nonchlorinated water that has become contaminated. Botulism can be caught if the bacteria enters your body through an open cut or sore. Salmonella can actually be caught by petting one's pet snake, turtle, lizard, or iguana. Reptiles are noted salmonella carriers, as are insects.

Who Gets Food Poisoning?

Anybody can get food poisoning, but the consequences can be much more serious in infants, young children, the elderly, pregnant women (who could miscarry), people with serious illnesses, and those whose immune systems are weak.

The majority of reported cases of food poisoning occur as individual cases. However, some of them might actually be part of widespread, but unrecognized, outbreaks. An outbreak occurs when a group of people eat the same contaminated food and two or more of them come down with the same illness. The group might have shared a meal at someone's house or might have purchased and eaten a contaminated product from the same store or restaurant.

Every year, around 500 outbreaks of food poisoning are reported to local and state health departments, which in turn report the cases to the Centers for Disease Control (CDC). Most of these outbreaks are local. A food poisoning outbreak is identified when a group of people realize that some or all of them became sick after a meal, and someone notifies the local health department. Increasingly, outbreaks are becoming more widespread, with individuals in different regions, states, or provinces coming down with the same infection, sometimes over a period of several weeks. A recent example is a salmonella outbreak that originated with a breakfast cereal produced in a Minnesota factory. The bacteria from this one food infected people in various American states over a period of several months before the CDC was notified and the food was recalled.

How to Report Food Poisoning

If you have experienced a case of food poisoning, one of the first things you will want to do is report the incident. Your report will ensure that the proper health authorities will be able to monitor any food manufacturers or establishments that are selling contaminated food to the public. In some cases, your action might cause an entire shipment of spoiled ground beef or improperly canned tuna to be recalled, taken off the shelves of stores and supermarkets, and destroyed. Ultimately, most of what we know about food poisoning and the bacteria that cause it stems from concerned consumers who have spoken out and reported outbreaks. Once a case is reported, an investigation takes place. A full investigation can involve specialists ranging from epidemiologists, microbiologists, and food scientists to veterinarians and factory engineers.

If you have a problem with any kind of meat, poultry, or egg product—you find a tooth in the middle of your packaged hot dog, or mold in your canned chili, for example—call the toll-free United States Department of Agriculture (USDA) Meat and Poultry

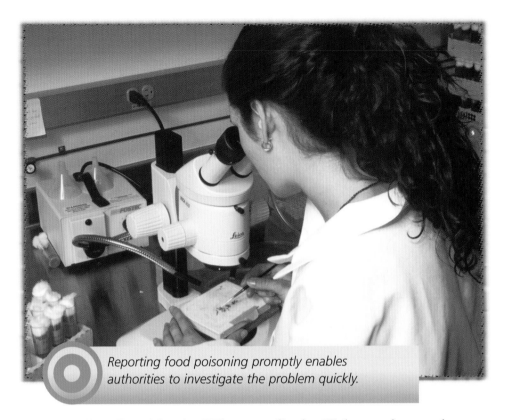

Reporting food poisoning promptly enables authorities to investigate the problem quickly.

Hotline listed in the Where to Go for Help section at the back of this book. To report problems concerning any other kinds of food products—a dead cockroach in your cereal box, for example—get in touch with the Food and Drug Administration (FDA). To find an FDA office in your area, look in your phone book under United States Government, under the Health and Human Services section.

When making your complaint, you'll need to provide the following information:

◉ **The brand name of the product**

◉ **The manufacturer of the product**

◎ The name and location of the store where the food product was purchased

◎ The date of purchase

If possible, keep the original container, packaging, and any uneaten portion of the food (freeze it). If you got sick as a result of consuming this contaminated food, you will need to provide specific details about the nature of your illness. If you do not want to make a formal complaint to the USDA or FDA, you should at least inform the store where you purchased the food or contact the product's manufacturer. If you got food poisoning from a meal you ate in a restaurant, contact the restaurant manager and alert him or her to the situation. Doing so will save others from illness, or even death. It will also help identify new strains of bacteria and enable specialists to better prevent, and even cure, food-related illnesses.

Chapter 2

When You Get Food Poisoning

After you swallow contaminated food, there is a delay—called the incubation period—before you experience symptoms. This delay can range from two hours to several days, depending on what kind of bacteria was in the food you ate and how much contaminated food you consumed. During the incubation period, the bacteria move through your stomach and into your intestine. Attaching themselves to the walls of your intestine, they begin to reproduce. Some bacteria stay in the intestinal walls, some invade other tissues, and some produce a toxin that is released into your blood. Depending on the quantity of contaminated food that you ate, and the type and toxicity of the bacteria, symptoms can range from mild to severe.

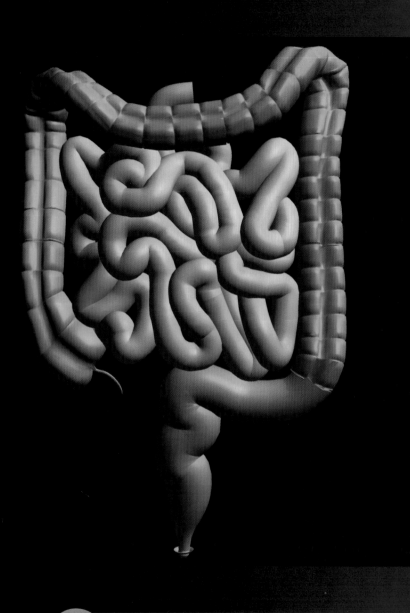

After they're eaten, bacteria move through the stomach and intestines, where they reproduce.

See How They Grow

All foods contain bacteria, but when proper precautions are taken, it is far less likely that an illness will occur. A particularly common mistake is leaving food out overnight. Because a single bacterium reproduces by dividing itself every half hour, in twelve hours, a bacterium can produce sixteen million toxic offspring.

Major Symptoms

The first indication that you might have food poisoning is often a growing feeling of nausea. This usually leads to throwing up, which is frequently accompanied by abdominal cramps. You might get diarrhea as well. Other common symptoms include fever, chills, weakness, and headaches. Most common cases of food poisoning do not last longer than twenty-four to forty-eight hours. More serious varieties of food poisoning, such as salmonella and *E. coli,* could take anywhere from a few days to a week to run their course.

Less common but far more dangerous types of food poisoning often cause additional symptoms that are much more severe. Botulism, for example, which affects approximately 20 adults and 250 infants a year, causes

What Is Nausea?

Nausea is the feeling you get preceding the urge to throw up. When you throw up, or vomit, whatever is in your stomach is forced up through your esophagus and out of your mouth. If you vomit a lot, you should try to drink as many liquids as possible. Try slowly sipping clear fluids, such as water or ginger ale (the flatter, the better) a little bit at a time so as not to upset your stomach.

a dry mouth, difficulties in speaking and swallowing, double vision, and breathing problems that could lead to respiratory failure. These symptoms take between eight and thirty-six hours to appear. The dinoflagellate that causes shellfish poisoning affects the human nervous system, and symptoms include muscle weakness, lightheadedness, numbness and a tingling sensation around the mouth and face, paralysis of the arms and legs, and breathing problems, as well as the more common nausea, cramps, and vomiting.

Severe salmonella poisoning is characterized by muscle pain and extreme diarrhea, as well as the more usual symptoms of upset stomach and dry mouth. Unfortunately, these conditions—particularly the diarrhea—can last for up to a week, or even two.

What Is Diarrhea?

Also called "the runs," diarrhea is a common condition. As you probably know, it is characterized by the frequent need to relieve yourself of fecal matter that is usually extremely liquid. Most diarrhea is caused by infections that are the result of consuming contaminated food or water.

Although it can be uncomfortable and embarrassing (particularly when you are not in the privacy of your own home), you should not try to stop diarrhea by taking medication right away. This is because diarrhea, like throwing up, is the body's way of getting rid of whatever bacteria or virus is infecting your body. Usually, diarrhea comes on suddenly and will stop by itself, without any treatment, in a day or two. However, diarrhea that lasts for more than a few days, is particularly explosive or bloody, and is accompanied by pain, a high fever, or chills is serious and requires immediate medical attention.

Remember that symptoms can take up to forty-eight hours to appear.

Diagnosis

As we saw in chapter 1, food poisoning is good at disguising itself. It is sometimes difficult to determine if indeed you do have food poisoning, particularly in cases where the effects of food contamination might take twenty-four hours or more to appear.

Aside from the presence of the symptoms mentioned earlier, there are other ways of diagnosing food poisoning. An obvious step you can take is to check with people who ate the same foods and see if any of them also became sick. Another step you can take is to have food examined in a laboratory to verify if either bacteria or toxins are present. Having a blood sample analyzed, or a stool culture taken and analyzed is also a good idea.

What Is a Stool Culture?

When you have food poisoning or any other type of related illness, the best way of determining what bacteria are infecting you is by having a doctor take a sample of your stool (feces) to send to a lab. In the lab, the sample is isolated in a culture atmosphere, i.e., a controlled environment that favors the growth of microorganisms. In this way, bacterial growth can be observed and contaminating organisms can be identified.

Complications

Last year, Julie, her mom—who was seven months pregnant—and her dad celebrated the fourth of July weekend by going to not one, but three big parties. Little did Julie's family know that that weekend would change their lives forever.

On the morning of July 9, Julie's mom began feeling fluish. Both Julie and her dad left for work and Julie's mom was in bed. When Julie came home from the store at the end of the afternoon, her mom was still in bed, moaning. She told Julie that she was experiencing horrible cramps and that she was bleeding. Worried about the baby, Julie's mom had called her gynecologist who said that stomach flu couldn't hurt the baby and that some bleeding was normal. But the bleeding and the cramps were getting worse.

Julie called her dad who came home immediately. They drove Julie's mom to her gynecologist. The doctor listened to the baby's heartbeat and looked worried. She told Julie's dad that her mom had to go to the emergency room immediately. At the hospital, doctors said that the baby's heart was racing. Something was terribly wrong. A life-threatening infection had attacked Julie's mom. Labor would have to be induced that night or the baby would die.

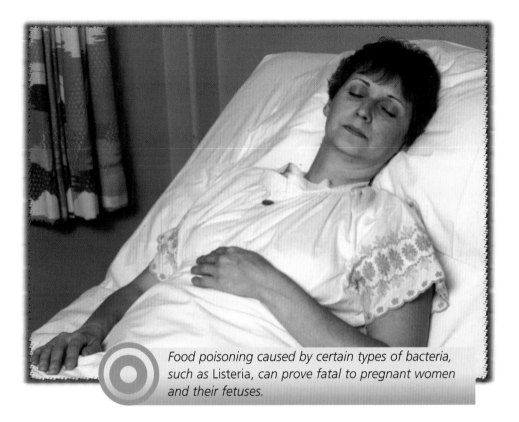

Food poisoning caused by certain types of bacteria, such as Listeria, can prove fatal to pregnant women and their fetuses.

That night, Julie's mom gave birth to a tiny baby boy named Patrick. He was purple and needed to be incubated immediately. Baby Patrick was alive for almost two days. Julie's mom was devastated, but she became really hysterical when the doctors told her about the infection that had made her sick and had killed Patrick: Listeria. *None of the doctors knew much about* Listeria, *but they said it came from something Julie's mom had eaten. Julie's mom couldn't stop crying. She said Patrick's death was her fault.*

At home, Julie searched for information about Listeria *on the Internet. She discovered that the*

bacteria could be found in any kind of fresh produce but that it is often found in processed foods such as potato salad or hot dogs. Julie thought about all the potato salad and hot dogs they had eaten the previous weekend. Reading on, she also discovered that most pregnant women who get infected by Listeria *die. She realized that her mom was really lucky not to have been one of them.*

Most cases of food poisoning are mild in nature and pass quickly. However, certain types of bacteria, as well as severe and prolonged cases of food poisoning, can lead to complications. One of the most frequent complications is dehydration. You become dehydrated when your body lacks the fluids necessary for it to function normally.

Look Out for Symptoms That Become Severe

Dehydration can be caused by losing too many liquids or by not drinking enough. You risk becoming dehydrated when you vomit, have diarrhea, or sweat excessively. In the case of food poisoning, where both vomiting and diarrhea can be severe, the threat of dehydration can be a problem.

Losing 5 percent of your body fluids is considered a mild loss; up to 10 percent is deemed moderate; but up to 15 percent and over can seriously threaten your health. If not treated quickly, severe dehydration can lead to seizures, cardiovascular failure, permanent brain damage, and even death.

Other symptoms that are severe or last for an exceptionally long period require medical attention. These include:

- ◎ **The presence of blood (in stools or vomit)**
- ◎ **Black vomit**
- ◎ **A high fever (temperature of over 101.5°F)**
- ◎ **Problems retaining fluids for more than ten hours**
- ◎ **Problems breathing**
- ◎ **Severe abdominal pain**
- ◎ **Diarrhea that lasts for more than four days**
- ◎ **Inability to swallow**
- ◎ **Seizures**

Chapter 3

Recovering from Food Poisoning

Even with mild cases of food poisoning, the three most common symptoms—nausea, throwing up, and diarrhea—get in the way of your day-to-day functioning. Because of the fever and weakness that accompany food poisoning, it is best to stay at home in bed, or somewhere within close proximity to a bathroom.

Liquids and Fluids

There is no real medication that can cure you of food poisoning. Once you have it, you pretty much have to live through it. The fact that you will have diarrhea and will be throwing up means that it would be virtually useless to take oral medications. These will be expelled immediately and can even increase feelings of nausea. Also, although unpleasant, diarrhea and vomiting are actually natural and efficient ways of cleansing your body of whatever is contaminating you.

Of course, as we saw in the last chapter, too much vomiting or diarrhea can be dangerous. To avoid this, you should make sure, as mentioned earlier, to drink plenty of clear liquids at regular intervals (such as every twenty minutes). If dehydration is severe, your doctor or pharmacist might suggest oral rehydration. This consists of taking electrolytes, a liquid solution made up of various chemicals including salt, which helps to rehydrate the body's essential fluids and replenish minerals.

For extremely serious dehydration, intravenous rehydration might be necessary. During this process, medications or fluids are injected into your blood with a needle. Although this can sometimes be done at your doctor's office, in more urgent cases hospitalization might be necessary.

Antidiarrheals

Although a little diarrhea is not harmful, too much can be extremely uncomfortable. Taking over-the-counter medications such as Pepto-Bismol, Imodium, and Kaopectate will help solidify your stool and will sometimes reduce the frequency with which you have to go to the bathroom. For more serious cases, your doctor can prescribe stronger antidiarrheals such as codeine and loperamide.

In terms of natural remedies, certain bulk foods will cause your stool to thicken and will cut down on your urge to eliminate. The most efficient of these are rice, bananas, yogurt, cheese, and fibrous foods such as bread or cereals containing whole wheat and bran. Meanwhile, stay away from coffee, milk, and any kind of fatty food—these will increase diarrhea, upset your stomach, and provoke nausea.

Serious Cases of Food Poisoning

Most of the time, the type of food poisoning you get will be fairly mild and simple to deal with. Within twelve to twenty-four hours, most of the major symptoms will have passed and you will be well on your way to recovery. However, if by chance you are infected with one of the much rarer but much more serious forms of food poisoning, immediate medical care or hospitalization will be necessary.

Botulism, for example, threatens your respiratory system, making breathing difficult. If left untreated, you have a 70 percent chance of dying, so it is essential that you get to the closest hospital emergency room immediately in order to begin respiratory treatment. This usually involves a process known as intubation, where a tube is inserted through your nose or mouth and into your trachea (the tube that transports air to your lungs) to provide an airway for oxygen. If you have difficulty swallowing, you will probably be given fluids intravenously. At the same time, you need to take a botulinus antitoxin in order to kill the dangerous bacterial toxins in your system.

A trip to the emergency room is also essential if you suspect that you have shellfish poisoning. If possible, try to bring the contaminated shellfish with you when you go to the hospital. In serious cases, treatment could include having your stomach pumped (gastric lavage) to remove any poison, getting a cathartic (which cleans out your bowels), or receiving intubation in the event that you are experiencing trouble breathing. Although shellfish poisoning can be serious, it is rarely fatal.

One night, when she had to work late, Raul's mom asked him to baby-sit his little brother, Tim. She had left lots of food in the fridge so that Raul could cook dinner. Raul was a vegetarian, but Tim loved meat, so Raul grilled him a couple of hamburgers. The first ones he burnt to a crisp because the heat was too high, and Tim refused to eat them.

"Fine," grumbled Raul as he shaped another patty. "This time I'll barely cook them at all."

A few days later, Tim was sent home from school because he was running a fever. By evening, his temperature had shot up to 102°F, and he felt awful. Mrs. Shabaz gave Tim some

Botulism in Texas—a Serious Case

A recent outbreak of botulism in El Paso, Texas, was the fourth largest outbreak of this disease in the United States. What made it go down in history was not the fact that twenty-three people were contaminated, but that the symptoms were so strange. Aside from the usual nausea and diarrhea, there were brain-related problems such as blurred vision, slurred speech, and dizziness.

When the outbreak was reported, the CDC immediately began investigating. It discovered that the food poisoning was caused by eating a homemade potato-based dip. The nasty culprit responsible for the actual poisoning were foil-wrapped baked potatoes that had been left out at room temperature. Although the chef who prepared the dip swore that the wrapped and baked potatoes had been left out only overnight (eighteen hours), CDC botulism experts concluded that the chef was lying.

After numerous tests, it was proven that it takes at least three days for

This merganser, one of 8,000 water birds estimated to have been killed by an outbreak of botulism in Hamburg, NY in December 2000, lies dead on the Lake Erie shore.

potatoes in such conditions to produce the deadly toxin. Although baking potatoes kill vegetative cells, botulism spores survive. Wrapped in foil (without oxygen) and left at room temperature, the spores grow and produce a poison that is one of the most deadly in nature. If the potatoes had been kept hot or been refrigerated, they would never have caused illness.

Tylenol and he went to sleep. But in the middle of the night, Raul and his mom were awakened by screaming. They ran into Tim's room and found him in bed. He was throwing up and having diarrhea at the same time.

With Raul driving and Mrs. Shabaz holding Tim, they drove to the hospital. Tim was having bloody diarrhea every five minutes and was crying in pain. At the hospital, the doctors immediately realized how serious Tim's condition was. They needed to give him fluids intravenously to save him from severe dehydration. The doctors tried to test Tim for shigella and salmonella but there was too much blood in his stool to take a proper stool culture. Tim kept getting worse, and nobody knew what was wrong. He was having bloody diarrhea every three minutes, day and night.

Finally, a pediatric gastroenterologist was called in from another city. He diagnosed E. coli *and began giving Tim blood transfusions. For the next few days, Tim stayed in the hospital, getting blood transfusions and receiving food and drink intravenously. Luckily, he made it through the ordeal. The day Tim sat up and asked to eat a hamburger, Raul, their mom, and all the nurses burst out laughing. Instead of the burger, however, they brought him a (very well-cooked) piece of chicken.*

Chapter 4

Food Safety at Home

Many people imagine that food poisoning is something you get when traveling in foreign countries, from restaurants or take-out food, or from the cafeteria at school. However, you might be surprised to discover that most cases of food poisoning take place in the supposed safety and cleanliness of people's own homes.

You might think that shopping for, preparing, storing, and cooking food is your parents' responsibility. Yet how many times have you run to the grocery store, defrosted hamburger meat, boiled an egg, packed your own lunch for school, made a sandwich, helped prepare and serve dinner, or wrapped and put away leftovers? If done improperly, any one of these seemingly simple tasks could conceivably lead to you or someone else in your family coming down with a case of food poisoning. It is essential for all members of a household to be responsible and to know how to store, handle, prepare, and serve food safely.

Shopping

In general, food in the United States is packed and stored according to strict health regulations. However, it never hurts to take certain precautions when you are shopping for food.

◎ Go shopping when you can take the food home right afterward. Food that sits in the backseat or trunk of a car can get hot and will spoil.

◎ Always check expiration dates of the food you buy.

◎ Do not buy canned goods with dents, bulges, or leakage.

◎ Avoid unpasteurized milk, cheeses, and fruit juices.

◎ Buy perishable food such as meat, eggs, milk, fruit, and vegetables last since they will start spoiling first.

◎ Separate meat, fish, seafood, and eggs from other food in your shopping cart and shopping bags. These foods have bacteria that can spread to other foods.

To ensure that the food you buy is safe for consumption, be sure to always check the expiration date.

Storing Food

As soon as you get home from the supermarket or grocery store, put everything away immediately, starting with fresh products, frozen foods, and all other foods that require refrigeration. All meat, poultry, fish, seafood, eggs and egg products, and milk and milk products should be refrigerated right away. Do not let meats and fish sit in plastic or bags. Their juices can leak and drip down, contaminating food on other shelves. It is best to transfer such goods into plastic storage containers or to wrap them safely in plastic or tin foil.

Refrigeration is essential for preserving food and preventing bacteria from growing. Make sure that the

Keeping the food in your refrigerator cold enough is vital in protecting against food poisoning.

temperature of your fridge is set at forty degrees Fahrenheit and that your freezer is set at zero degrees Fahrenheit. Opening the door all the time will raise the temperature, so try to keep the fridge open for only short periods of time. And always make sure that the door is properly shut. Remember to keep the fridge clean. If you spill something or knock something over, clean up your mess. Don't leave it for somebody else to do.

Food Safety Facts

A recent nationwide survey found that many Americans ignore safe food practices in their homes. The following statistics are startling.

◎ Thirty-three percent prepare meals in ways considered unsafe (i.e., not washing hands and using the same tools and surfaces for raw meats and other foods).

◎ Fifty-three percent admit to eating raw foods of animal origin.

◎ The most careless cooks are young, highly-educated white men between the ages of eighteen and twenty-nine.

◎ The most careful cooks are older, non-white women, forty years and over who have a high school education or less.

Handling Food

Whenever you are going to be touching or preparing food, your hands should be clean. Everything you touch—from a doorknob to a light switch—is full of germs and bacteria. Running your hands under tap water is not enough. You need to scrub your hands vigorously with hot water and soap. If you or anyone else in your family is sick or is coming down with something, they should not be involved in food preparation. Even if you are not sick, but you feel a cough or sneeze coming on, turn your head away and cover your nose and mouth. Then wash your hands. In the meantime, as much as you might love your pets, they should not be allowed to hang around in the kitchen, particularly when there is cooking going on.

Any surfaces and tools you use—countertops, cutting boards, plates, knives, forks, blenders, etc.—should be cleaned after each use. If you use a fork, plate, knife, or cutting board for one kind of food, always wash it before bringing it into contact with another kind of food. This is especially important when you are preparing raw food that has lots of bacteria.

Of course, any kind of fresh food—especially fruits and vegetables—should be thoroughly washed. There is a risk that these foods contain bacteria and insects, or have been contaminated by dangerous chemicals from fertilizers and insecticides.

If you are defrosting frozen food, let it thaw in the fridge itself or place it in a thoroughly sealed plastic bag and leave it in cold water. Defrosting in a microwave is fine, too. However, you should never leave food out on the counter to thaw (even if it is covered) since it can easily become contaminated. For the same reason, once food is thawed, it should be cooked immediately.

Cooking Food

Bacteria such as *Listeria* and *Salmonella* often live in animals' intestines. Thoroughly cook meat and eggs to ensure that any dangerous bacteria are killed. Delicious as they might be, if you eat a steak that is cooked rare, a soft-boiled egg, raw oysters, sushi, or other such dishes, you do run a risk of coming down with food poisoning. For this reason, avoid recipes that call for raw or partially cooked eggs.

Don't Lick the Batter or the Bowl

Foods that contain raw eggs, such as cake batter, mayonnaise, eggnog, meringues, custards, puddings, and homemade ice cream carry a risk of bacteria such as *Salmonella*. Because commercial versions of these products are made with pasteurized eggs that have been heated to kill bacteria, supermarket ice cream and major brands of mayonnaise are safe. However, even something as innocent (and pleasant) as eating homemade cookie dough or licking the batter in a cake pan could be problematic.

Cooking food thoroughly means two things: cooking for a certain amount of time and at a certain temperature—both of which will guarantee that your meat will be risk-free. In order to do this successfully, you need to have a food thermometer in your kitchen. Chances are you already do. Many North Americans use food thermometers when cooking big turkeys or hams for Thanksgiving or Easter. Interestingly enough, they don't use them the rest of the year. However, a (clean) thermometer—which measures the inside temperature of foods that are being cooked—is essential for determining whether meats, casseroles, cakes, and other foods are cooked all the way through.

One should be aware that raw eggs—often used in homemade baked goods—carry the risk of salmonella poisoning.

Make sure that your chicken is not pink, that seafood such as shrimps, lobsters, and prawns are bright red or pink, and that your fish is opaque (you cannot see through it) and flakes easily with a fork. If you're cooking food in a microwave, use a rotating turntable to ensure there are no cold spots during cooking. If your microwave is without a turntable, rotate the cooking dish by hand several times during cooking.

Storage

It is also important that you take care to store any cooked or prepared foods in the fridge or freezer.

Turning Up the Heat

Eating safely means cooking at the following temperatures:

Food	Internal Temperature
Ground Meat	
(i.e., hamburger meat)	165°F
Beef, Veal, Lamb	
Roasts/Steaks	
medium rare	145°F
medium	160°F
well-done	170°F
Pork Chops/Roasts/Ribs	
medium	160°F
well-done	170°F
Ham, fresh	160°F
Sausage, fresh	160°F
Poultry	
Chicken	
(whole and pieces)	180°F
Duck	180°F
Turkey (unstuffed, whole and pieces)	180°F
Stuffing (cooked separately)	165°F
Eggs	
Fried/Poached	yolks and whites must be firm
Casseroles	160°F
Sauces/Custards	160°F

Adapted from consumer guidelines of the U.S. Department of Agriculture (USDA) and the U.S. Food and Drug Administration (FDA).

Burger Bothers

New USDA research has discovered that color is not a foolproof indicator that meat has been cooked at a temperature high enough to kill bacteria such as *E. coli.* As a result, supermarkets have launched educational campaigns showing the importance of cooking with food thermometers. Recently, Wegmans Food Market set up special burger grilling demonstrations in its fifty-seven stores. These were accompanied by posters asking the question: "Which is done?" Below the caption were two burgers: one pink and one brown. The pink one, which had been cooked to 160°F, turned out to be the safely cooked one. The brown burger, cooked at only 140°F, could potentially contain all kinds of bacteria. Ultimately, hamburger meat can appear brown for all sorts of reasons, such as the amount of fat and water it contains. The only sure way to tell if your burger is done is by using a meat thermometer.

Storing food properly means wrapping it completely in plastic or foil or transferring it to a well-sealed glass or plastic container prior to refrigeration. Leaving food out at room temperature for more than two hours—even if it is covered in the oven, being marinated in sauce, or sitting in a covered pan on the stove—carries a risk of bacteria growth.

If you or someone in your household has left food out for more than two hours, you should throw it out. Do not even think of taste-testing it. Even a spoonful of contaminated food can make you sick. In general, most cooked foods can be refrigerated safely for three to five days before they spoil. If in doubt, throw it out.

Mold

Mold is the greenish/bluish wool-like growth that begins to appear and expand on foodstuffs and organic products, particularly when damp. If you catch sight of mold on anything in (or out) of your fridge, throw it out.

Although wasting food is not a very good habit, it is not worth getting violently sick because you felt guilty about throwing out that small amount of expensive pasta salad or your grandmother's specially made chocolate mousse. If you suddenly stumble upon food you had completely forgotten about, do not hesitate to chuck it (without tasting it), particularly if it looks or smells odd.

A Cautionary Tale

When volleyball practice was over, Linda was starving. On her way home, she dropped by the apartment of her boyfriend, Barry. He was going to cook her dinner that night. He wasn't home from the market yet, but Linda had a spare key. Knowing that she'd never be able to hold out until dinner without a snack, Linda heaped some cream cheese with chives onto a bagel and wolfed it down. Barry got home about a half-hour later and began making dinner. By that time Linda was feeling as if she wanted to throw up.

"I don't know why my stomach feels so nauseous," she confessed to Barry, as she lay on the sofa, her body all clenched up. "All I had to eat was a bagel and some of that chive cream cheese."

"What chive cream cheese?" asked Barry, puzzled.

"The stuff in your fridge," moaned Linda.

"Linda, the only cream cheese I ever buy is plain. It must have been old and moldy!"

Chapter 5

Food Safety Outside the Home

Often, you cannot control where food has been, who has touched it, and the temperatures at which it has been cooked and stored. Nonetheless, by taking certain precautions and by being conscious of certain warning signs, you can definitely reduce your risks of acquiring food poisoning outside the home.

Picnics, Barbecues, and Other Outings

When it becomes warmer and vacation time rolls around, it is hard to resist the temptation of eating outdoors. Whether on the beach, in a park, or in your own backyard, picnics and barbecues are practically a North American tradition. However, a combination of many hands and mouths (and therefore the risk of many germs) and food left out unprotected for a long time in warm temperatures, make such occasions high risk situations for food poisoning.

If you are cooking, wrapping, and transporting your own food, you will want to ensure that it is safe for you and others to eat. It is a good idea to make all sandwiches, salads, hard-boiled eggs, and desserts containing eggs or dairy products well ahead of time so that they can be refrigerated or frozen. Do not take these foods out of the fridge or freezer until the last minute. Other perishable foods (such as cold cuts and cheeses) should receive the same treatment.

Foods that do not need to be refrigerated at all are an even better option for an outdoor meal. Fruits, vegetables, hard cheeses and sausages, canned meats and fish, potato chips, bread, cookies and crackers, as well as edibles that come in bottles or jars (olives, pickles, and peanut butter), are all safe and easy-to-carry options that have little risk of spoiling and do not need to be packed in a cooler.

The perishables mentioned above, as well as all raw meats, such as steaks, ribs, chops, hot dogs, hamburger patties, and chicken, should all be stored and transported in a well-chilled cooler. Coolers should be insulated with enough ice or gel packs to keep the food at 40°F. Take food straight from the fridge or freezer and pack it into the cooler. Do not let it sit out at room temperature, even for a short time.

When dining outdoors, it is important to store perishable items, such as meat and dairy, in a cool place.

Once you get to your picnic or barbecue destination, make sure the cooler is left in a shady place. Keep the lid closed and avoid repeatedly opening the cooler. As long as food stays cool, it is safe. If ice melts, however, and the temperature of the cooler goes down, throw any leftovers away. Otherwise, you can eat the leftovers.

Barbecue Tips

◉ Let coals get good and hot before cooking food (twenty to thirty minutes).

◉ Only take raw meat out of the cooler right before cooking.

◎ Grill precooked meat until it is steaming hot.

◎ Grill all meats—particularly hamburger meat—until thoroughly cooked.

◎ When taking food off the grill, put it on a different plate than the one that held the uncooked food.

School Lunches

Although millions of North American students buy their lunches at school cafeterias, millions more bring their lunch to school in lunch boxes or brown paper bags. Preparing, wrapping, and carrying around your lunch all day poses certain food poisoning risks.

If you are making your own lunch, be certain that all the food, cutlery, utensils, and wrapping you use are clean. It is also important to keep hot foods such as soups, chili, and stew as hot as possible for as long as possible by storing them—piping hot—in a thermos with a tightly screwed-on lid. Equally important is to keep perishable foods as cold as possible, for as long as possible. The best way to do this is to buy an insulated lunch box and to pack it with freezer gel packs.

Once you get to school, keep lunch bags and boxes out of the sunlight and away from radiators and other heat sources. Know that even insulated lunch boxes with gel packs will not keep food cool all day long. Any perishable foods you do not eat at lunch should be thrown out instead of being brought home or eaten as an after-school snack.

Restaurants

Most North American restaurants are very careful about maintaining a high level of food hygiene, especially since their very survival and success depend upon properly preparing and serving food. The last thing a restaurant wants is for a customer to come down with a case of food poisoning. This could seriously threaten its reputation and its business. Restaurants follow strict health guidelines that ensure that food on their premises is appropriately stored and handled. Health officials, who verify that these guidelines are being followed, regularly visit restaurants. If any irregularities are found, the restaurant can receive a warning or may even be closed temporarily if conditions such as refrigeration or cleanliness are considered to be unsafe.

Of course, even when eating out you should still take certain precautions. Always ask to have meat and eggs well cooked and be suspicious of any dish containing a dairy product such as milk or cream that tastes a little sour or off. If a plate, glass, tabletop, or piece of cutlery is dirty, ask for it to be cleaned. If a soup, stew, or chili— or anything else you suspect might have been sitting in a pot on the stove all day—is served to you lukewarm, ask that it be reheated so that it arrives steaming. And, obviously, any dish that comes garnished with any strange specks, strands of hairs, or insects should be sent back to the kitchen. If you get sick as a result of eating restaurant or take-out food, report the incident to your local health department.

Traveling

When traveling in foreign countries, you must always take special care with both food and water. First of all, in many countries, health regulations concerning food and hygiene are not always as rigidly followed as in North America and in many parts of Europe. Second, just as different countries and climates produce different plants and animals, they also produce different kinds of viruses, germs, and bacteria. Some of these might be dangerous. Others—particularly bacteria—although not dangerous, might leave you with nausea, diarrhea, or an upset stomach, simply because your body's digestive system is not used to them.

In tropical countries with hot climates, food gets warm and can spoil with alarming speed. And methods of keeping supplies cool are not always sufficient to avoid growth of harmful bacteria. As a result, the normal precautions you would take with the food you eat at home apply all the more when you are traveling. To be extra safe, however, keep the following tips in mind:

- ◉ Avoid salads, sandwiches, and other edibles made with mayonnaise (which spoils very quickly).

- ◉ Drink filtered or bottled water instead of tap water.

- ◉ Do not drink straight out of cans or bottles, use a straw.

- ◉ Make sure all meats, fish, seafood, and poultry are well cooked.

- ◉ Do not eat food from street vendors (unless a local friend assures you they are safe).

- ◉ Ask for drinks without ice (which could be made from unfiltered tap water).

- ◉ Fruit with skin you must peel off (mango, papaya, orange) is safer than fruit with edible skins (apples, berries) that might have come into contact with bacteria or other substances.

Conclusion

Recent surveys have shown that North Americans are becoming more aware of the dangers of food poisoning and safe ways of handling what they eat. Nonetheless, failure to properly cook and cool foods at home and in restaurants is still the leading cause of food poisoning outbreaks. Government health authorities, scientists, food manufacturers, restaurateurs, and consumer groups are all constantly striving to create safer food as well as safer conditions for packaging, storing, transporting, preparing, selling, and serving it. Although in general, they have been pretty successful, 9,000 deaths a year from food poisoning means that there is still progress to be made.

The main problem is that so many things about the food we eat are constantly changing. With an increase in travel, imports and exports, and new foods, bacteria are easily spread around the world and adapt to new circumstances. The environment, and nature itself, is constantly evolving. So are the ways that food is produced and consumed. Because of this, the effects of new strains of bacteria, as well as fertilizers, pesticides, and drugs given to plants and animals, need to be studied. Health regulations need to be updated and enforced. Consumer awareness and habits regarding food hygiene need to change. Hopefully, reading this book has increased your awareness and has changed the way you will handle, store, cook, and serve food. Now you will be equipped with the information you need to go out and help change the unsafe food-handling habits of the people around you.

Glossary

dehydration When the body is deprived of fluids.

diarrhea Extremely liquid fecal matter.

electrolytes Liquid solution that helps to rehydrate the body's essential fluids and to replenish minerals.

epidemiologist Scientist/doctor who studies distribution and control of disease in a population.

gastroenterologist Scientist/doctor who specializes in the stomach and intestines.

intubation Process in which a tube is inserted through the mouth or nose and into the trachea, allowing a person to breathe.

pasteurization Partial sterilization (through heat) of a substance or liquid that kills bacteria.

perishable Likely to spoil or decay.

spore One-celled microorganism that hooks up with other spores to form new microorganisms.

toxins Poisons.

For More Information

In the United States
Centers for Disease Control and Prevention (CDC)
National Center for Infectious Diseases
1600 Clifton Road
Atlanta, GA 30333
(800) 311-3435
Web site: http://www.cdc.gov/foodsafety

Federal Consumer Information Center (FCIC)
Dept. WWW
Pueblo, CO 81009
(800) 688-9889
Web site: http://www.pueblo.gsa.gov/food.htm

U.S. Department of Agriculture (USDA)
Food Safety and Inspection Service
14th and Independence Avenue S.W.
Washington, DC 20250-3700

(202) 720-2791
Web site: http://www.usda.gov/about.htm

U.S. Food and Drug Administration (FDA)
Center for Food Safety and Applied Nutrition
200 C Street SW
Washington, DC 20204
Toll-Free Information Line: (888) SAFE FOOD (723-3366)
Web site: http://vm.cfsan.fda.gov/list.htmlΔ

To Report a Case of Food Poisoning:
FDA's Food Information and Seafood Hotline
(888) SAFE FOOD

USDA's Meat and Poultry Hotline
(800) 535-4555

In Canada
Canadian Food Inspection Agency (CFIA)
59 Camelot Drive
Nepean, ON K1A 0Y9
(613) 225-2342
http://www.cfia-acia.agr.ca

The Canadian Partnership for Consumer Food
    Safety Education
75 Albert Street, Suite 1101
Ottawa, ON K1P 5E7
(613) 798-3042
http://www.canfightbac.org/english/index.shtml

For Further Reading

Cody, Mildred M. *Safe Food for You and Your Family.* New York: John Wiley & Sons, 1996.

Fox, Nicols. *It Was Probably Something You Ate.* New York: Penguin, 1999.

Lacey, Richard. *Poison on a Plate: The Dangers in the Food We Eat—and How to Avoid Them.* New York: Metro Books, 1999.

Latta, Sara L. *Food Poisoning and Foodborne Diseases.* Springfield, NJ: Enslow, 1999.

Matossian, Mary Kilbourne. *Poisons of the Past: Molds, Epidemics, and History.* New Haven, CT: Yale University Press, 1991.

Satin, Morton. *Food Alert! The Ultimate Source Book for Food Safety.* New York: Facts on File, Inc., 1999.

Scott, Elizabeth, and Paul Sockett. *How to Prevent Food Poisoning: A Practical Guide to Safe Cooking, Eating, and Food Handling.* New York: John Wiley & Sons, 1998.

Turkington, Carol A. *Protect Yourself from Contaminated Food and Drink.* New York: Ballantine Books, 1998.

Index

About the Author

Mick Isle has a degree in journalism from Trinity College in Dublin, Ireland.

Photo Credits

Cover by Maura Burochow; pp. 2, 39, 40, 44, 46, 51 by Antonio Mari; p. 7 by Maura Burochow; p. 10 © Conway Trefethen/FPG; p. 13 © Kalab/CMSP; p. 18 © Wedgwood/CMSP; p. 21 © Life Art; p. 27 © CMSP; p. 35 © Associated Press AP.

Series Design

Tom Forget

Layout

Danielle Goldblatt